A BULLY-FREE PARTY

Text by Pamela Hall
Illustrations by Bob Ostrom

magic wagon

Content Consultant
Finessa Ferrell, Director,
National Center for School Engagement

visit us at www.abdopublishing.com

Published by Magic Wagon, a division of the ABDO Group, PO Box 398166, Minneapolis, MN 55439. Copyright © 2013 by Abdo Consulting Group, Inc. International copyrights reserved in all countries. All rights reserved. No part of this book may be reproduced in any form without written permission from the publisher.

Printed in the United States of America, North Mankato, Minnesota.
032012
092012

 THIS BOOK CONTAINS AT LEAST 10% RECYCLED MATERIALS.

Text by Pamela Hall
Illustrations by Bob Ostrom
Edited by Holly Saari
Design and production by Craig Hinton

Library of Congress Cataloging-in-Publication Data

Hall, Pamela, 1961-
  A bully-free party / by Pamela Hall ; illustrated by Bob Ostrom ; content consultant, Finessa Ferrell.
      p. cm. -- (A bully-free world)
  ISBN 978-1-61641-845-8
  1. Bullying--Juvenile literature. 2. Bullying--Prevention--Juvenile literature. 3. Parties--Juvenile literature. 4. Aggressiveness in children--Juvenile literature. I. Ostrom, Bob. II. Title.
  BF637.B85H336 2013
  302.34'3--dc23
                                    2011038552

TABLE OF CONTENTS

BULLYING
AT A PARTY

Why are some people bullies? Bullies are usually angry people. They make others feel bad. Bullies feel better about themselves when they hurt others. They do this by hitting and punching. They also hurt others by name-calling or spreading rumors.

It is hard to stay away from bullies at a party. Lots of people are together at once. Bullies want to ruin other people's fun. The kids at Taylor's birthday party are bullying each other. Let's see how they stop the bullying!

5

INVITED
BULLIES

Taylor's mom made Taylor invite Carlos to his party. She didn't want Carlos to be left out. But Carlos is the biggest bully in class. Taylor thinks Carlos is just too mean. He doesn't want to talk to him at his party. What should he do?

WHAT TO DO

First, Taylor should tell his mom that Carlos is a bully. His mom can talk to Carlos's mom. If Carlos acts mean, he will be sent home.

Second, Taylor should try to be nice to Carlos. Taylor knows it hurts to be left out. Sometimes kids bully because they feel alone. Maybe Carlos just needs a friend.

One out of every four kids who bully will end up in trouble with the police when they grow up. Carlos might stop bullying when he feels like part of the group.

BEING MEAN

Verbal bullying is when someone says something mean in order to hurt another person. Words can hurt as much as punches and kicks. Being called a name or being made fun of makes people feel bad.

Derek made fun of Taylor and his party. Taylor feels bad now. Can anyone stop Derek from bullying? Yes they can!

WHAT TO DO

Sarah heard Derek be mean to Taylor. About one-third of all kids are bullied at some point. Sarah wants to be an upstander. Standing up to someone who bullies is one of the best ways to stop bullying.

Sarah could make a joke of what Derek said. Or, she can tell Derek he is wrong.

PEER PRESSURE

When kids try to get other kids to do things they don't want to do, it is called peer pressure. Joe and Tim are eating cake at the party. Joe is usually nice. But even nice people sometimes bully. About six out of ten kids will be bullies at some point.

Joe wants to make Tim do something he doesn't want to do. What can Tim do?

WHAT TO DO

First, Tim can make a joke out of it. He could say, "Why should I go put frosting in Emily's hair? It would look much better in yours."

Another thing Tim can do is change the subject. If Joe gets interested in something else, he might forget all about the frosting.

WHISPERED SECRETS

Social bullying is when a bully leaves a person out on purpose to be hurtful. Social bullying is also telling secrets in front of other kids and spreading rumors. Girls do this more than boys. Many girls put others down so they feel better about themselves.

Emily whispers a mean secret to Ava about Lee. It would hurt Lee's feelings. What should Isabel do when she hears Emily?

WHAT TO DO

Isabel should be an upstander and help Lee. She should look right at Emily. She should be firm. Isabel should say, "Stop saying those things. They are not true." Then Isabel can say something nice about Lee's outfit. Saying the opposite of Emily will make Emily look silly.

TAKE THE
BULLY TEST

How can you tell if you ever bully? You are a bully if you do things you know will hurt people or make them feel bad. Ask yourself these questions:

Q Do I feel better when I hurt other kids or take their stuff?

Q Do I use my strength or size to get my way?

Q Do I like to leave others out to make them feel bad?

Q Have I ever spread a rumor that I knew was not true?

Q Do I like teasing others?

Q Is it funny to me when I see other kids getting made fun of?

Q Have I ever kicked, punched, or hit someone?

If you answered "yes" to any of these questions, you might be a bully. Is that really how you want to be?

Of course not! Everyone makes mistakes. You can change the way you act. The first step is to say, "I'm sorry." Practice being nice to other people. Think before you say or do something. Treat others the way you want to be treated.

NOTE TO PARENTS AND CAREGIVERS

Young children often imitate their parents' or caregivers' behaviors. If you show bullying actions or use bullying language, it is likely your children will, too. They do not know their behavior is unacceptable because they see it in trusted adults. You can help prevent your student from bullying by modeling good behavior.

WORDS TO KNOW

peer pressure—a feeling that you must act in the same way as others in order for them to like you.

rumor—talk that may not be true but is repeated by many people.

social bullying—telling secrets, spreading rumors, giving mean looks, and leaving kids out on purpose.

upstander—someone who sees bullying and stands up for the person being bullied.

verbal bullying—being mean to someone using words, such as by name-calling.

WEB SITES

To learn more about bullying at a party, visit ABDO Group online at **www.abdopublishing.com**. Web sites about bullying at a party are featured on our Book Links page. These links are routinely monitored and updated to provide the most current information available.